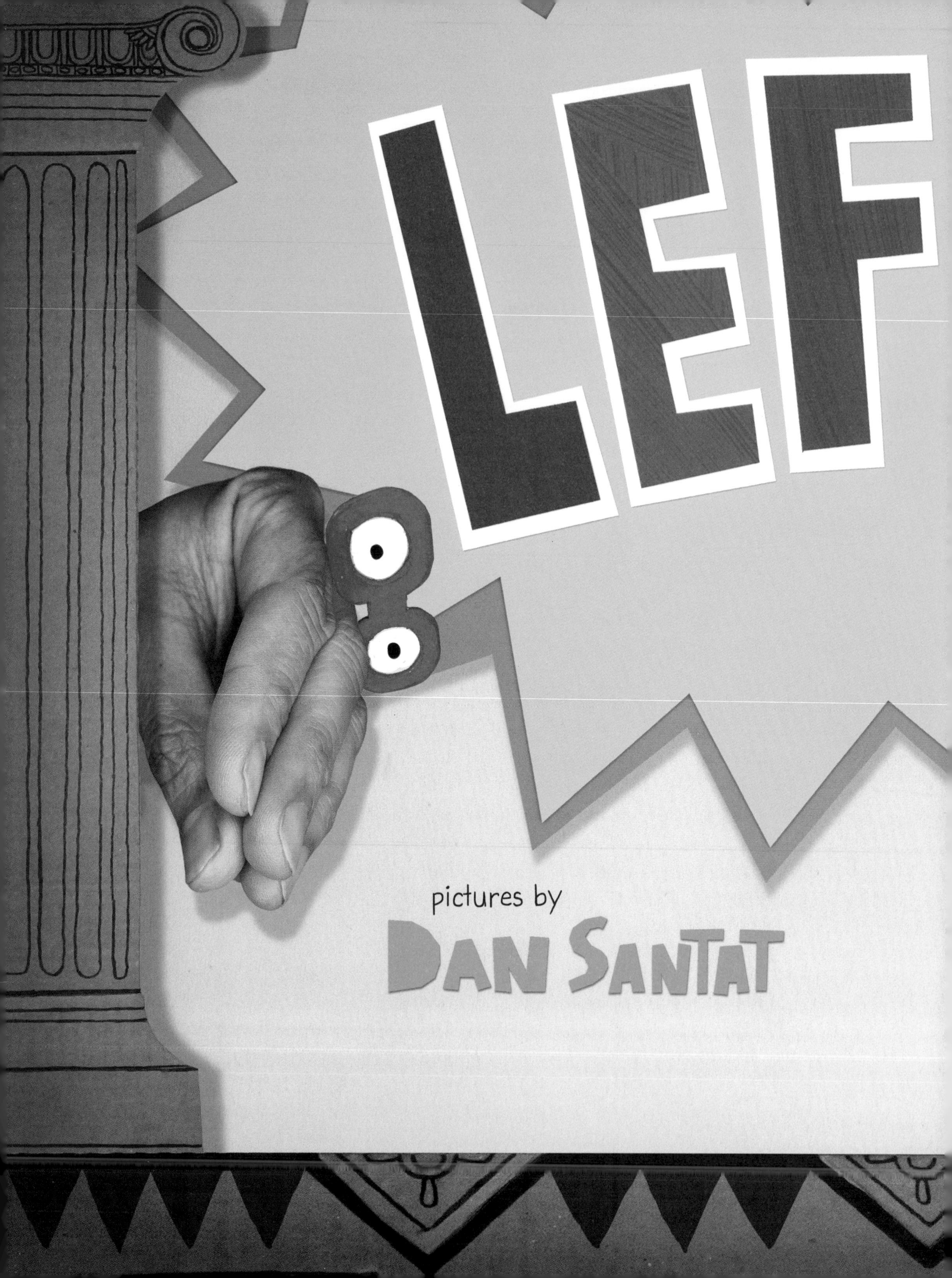
LEF
pictures by
DAN SANTAT

TY

A Story That Is Not All Right

words by

Mo Willems

union
square
kids

NEW YORK

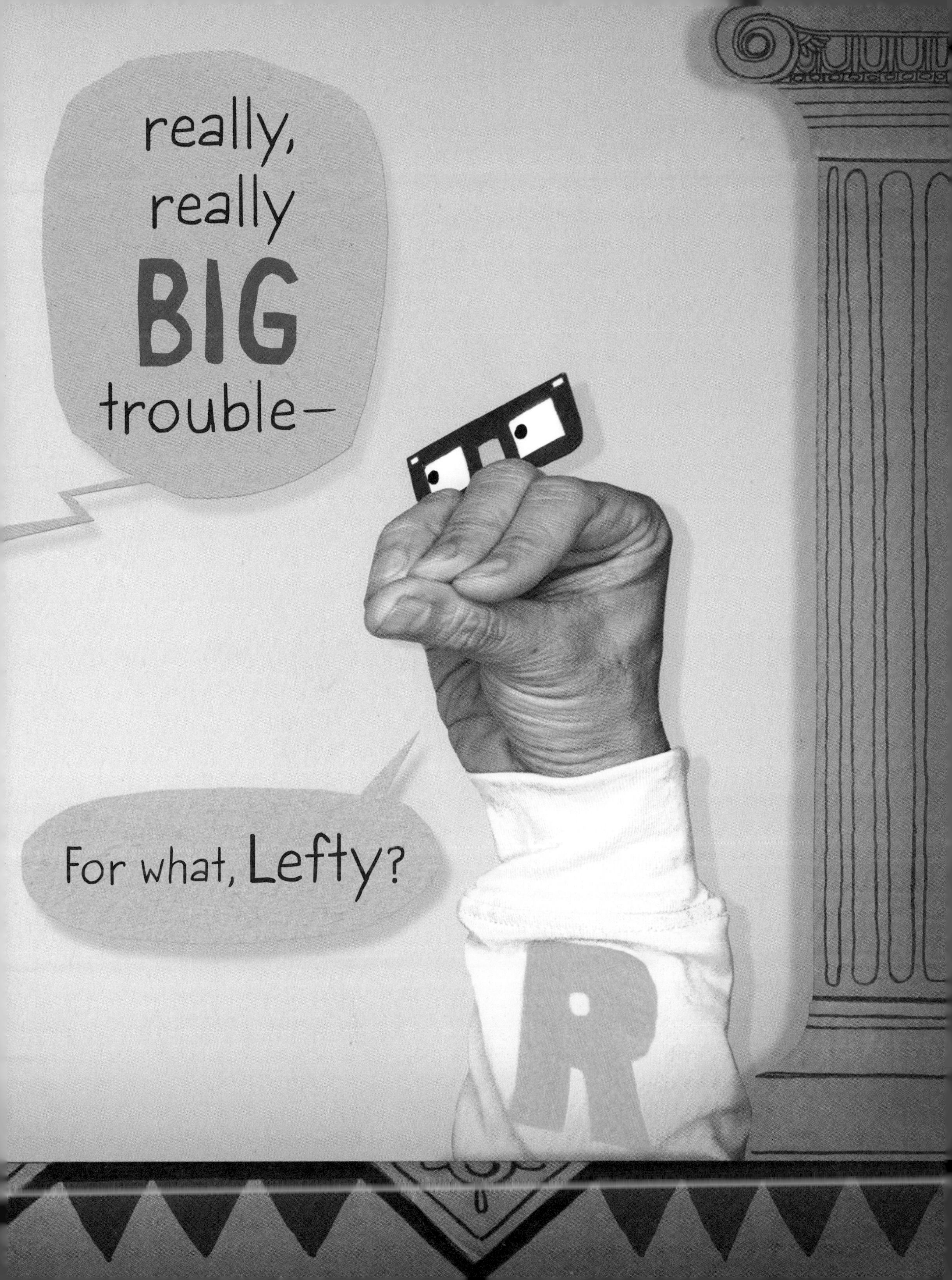
really, really BIG trouble—
For what, Lefty?

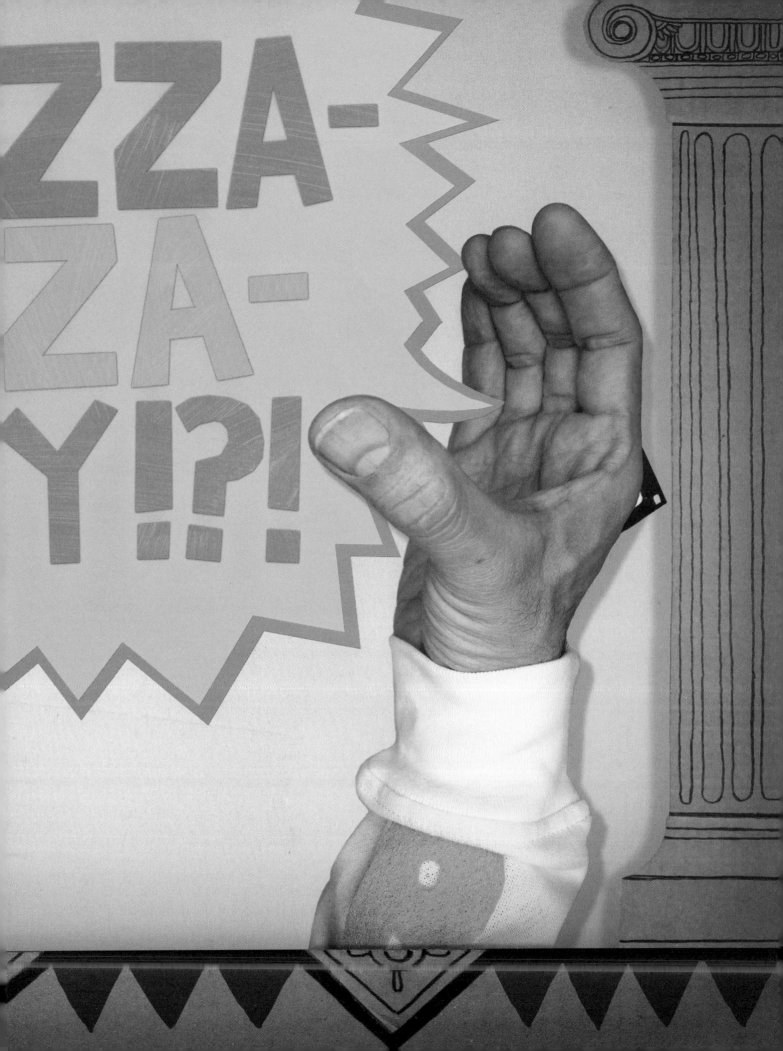

I HAVE **NO IDEA.**

EVEN IN ANCIENT TIMES,
LEFT-HANDED PEOPLE PRETENDED
TO BE WHO THEY WEREN'T AND HID
THEIR LEFT-HANDEDNESS.

OR ELSE THEY WOULD BE LEFT OUT.

Over time, people slowly started to see that it's
not right to say it's wrong to be left-handed.

They left that old idea behind.

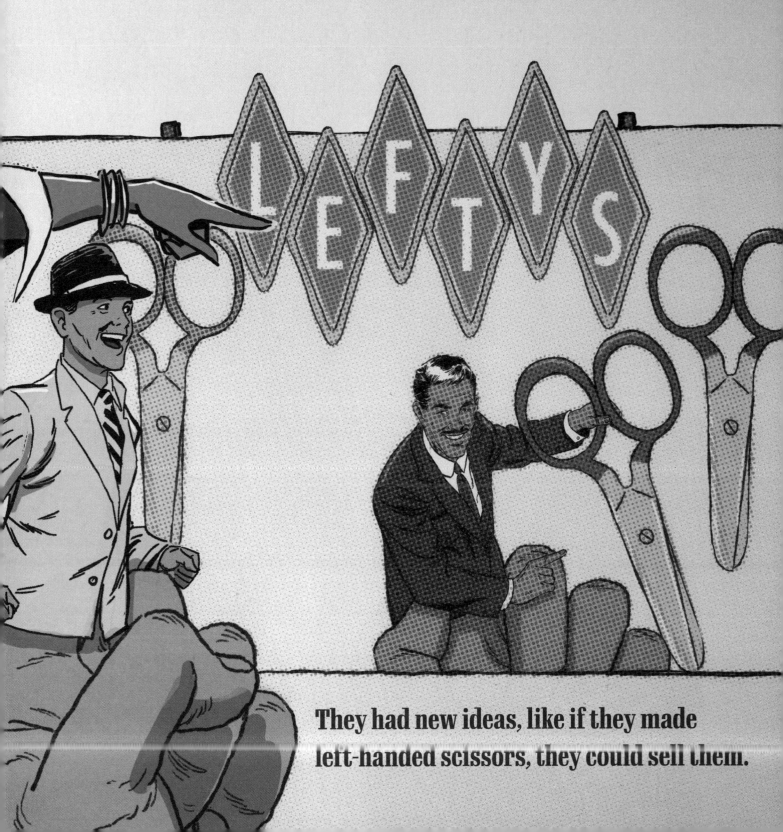

They had new ideas, like if they made
left-handed scissors, they could sell them.

Some left-handed people become famous.

Some right-handed people become famous.

FRIDA KAHLO

ABRAHAM LINCOLN

Some left-handed people do **NOT** become famous.

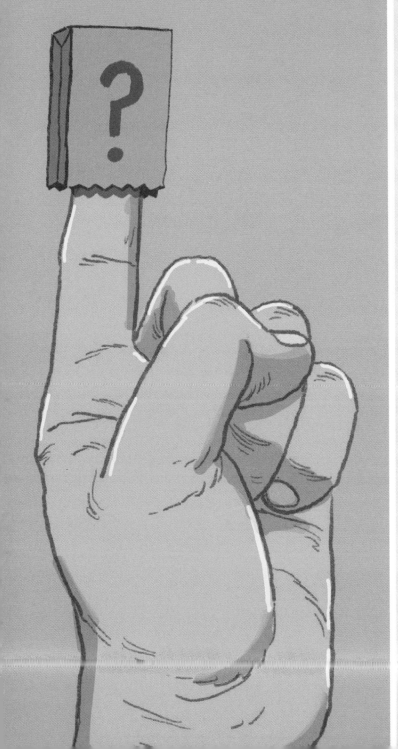

Some right-handed people do **NOT** become famous.

Some left-handed people are really, really nice.

Some right-handed people are really, really nice.

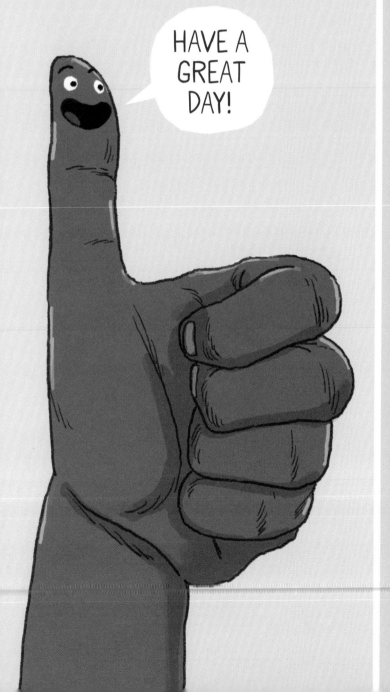

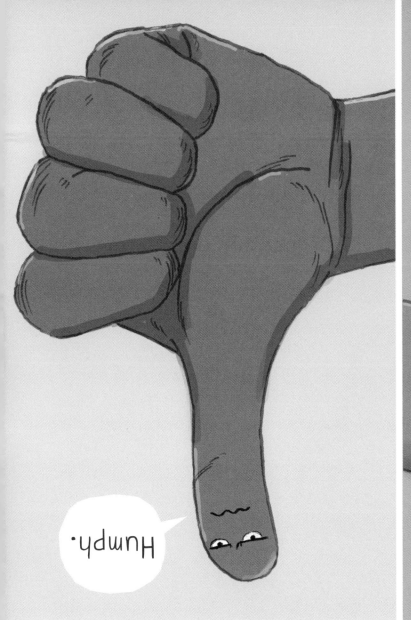

Other left-handed
people could work
on being nicer.

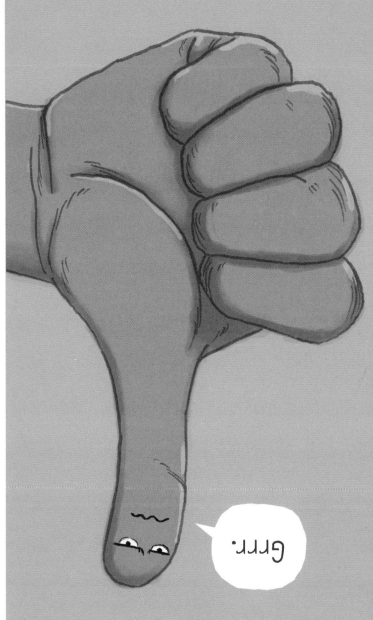

Other right-handed
people could also work
on being nicer.

union square kids

NEW YORK

UNION SQUARE KIDS and the distinctive Union Square Kids
logo are trademarks of Union Square & Co., LLC.
Union Square & Co., LLC, is a subsidiary of Sterling Publishing Co., Inc.

Specific House

A Specific House book.

HC ISBN: 978-1-4549-5148-3
BNE ISBN: 978-1-4549-5928-1

Library of Congress Cataloging-in-Publication Data

Names: Willems, Mo, author. | Santat, Dan, illustrator.
Title: Lefty / words Mo Willems ; pictures Dan Santat.
Description: New York : UNSQ Kids, 2024. | Audience: Ages 4-8 |
Summary: "A nonfiction narrative book about left-handedness"— Provided by publisher.
Identifiers: LCCN 2024000348 | ISBN 9781454951483 (hardcover)
Subjects: LCSH: Left- and right-handedness—Juvenile literature.
Classification: LCC GN233 .W55 2024 | DDC 152.3/35—dc23/eng/20240110
LC record available at https://lccn.loc.gov/2024000348

For information about custom editions, special sales, and premium purchases,
please contact specialsales@unionsquareandco.com.

Printed in Malaysia

Lot #:
2 4 6 8 10 9 7 5 3 1
08/24

unionsquareandco.com
mowillemsworkshop.com

Design by Dan Santat and Amelia Mack
This book text is set in UNSQ Sans, Danvetica, Herb, Greek Freak,
and Gimlet. Additional hand-lettering by Dan Santat.